The Cross-With-Us
RHINOCEROS

A Red Fox Book

Published by Random House Children's Books
20 Vauxhall Bridge Road, London SW1V 2SA

A division of Random House UK Ltd
London Melbourne Sydney Auckland
Johannesburg and agencies throughout the world

1 3 5 7 9 10 8 6 4 2

First published in Great Britain by Hutchinson Children's Books 1988
Beaver edition 1989
First Red Fox edition 1991
This Red Fox edition 1999

Printed in Hong Kong by Midas Printing Ltd

RANDOM HOUSE UK Limited Reg. No. 954009

ISBN 0 09 959800 0

The Cross-With-Us RHINOCEROS

John Bush *and* Paul Geraghty

RED FOX

To Pat and Garth

There was Willy, there was Wally, there was Tilly, there was I;
Four fine brave adventurers, beneath a bright blue sky.

We were full of fun and laughter until Tilly turned and said,
'What's that Willy? Look there Wally! What's that up ahead?'

We looked. We blinked. We looked again. We blinked. It was still there –

A huge great, grey rhinoceros, sniffing at the air.

He cocked his ears. He dropped his head. A huge foot pawed the ground.
And then that rhino turned on us and started charging down.

'I think that great rhinoceros is very, very cross with us;
VERY VERY cross with us,' said I.
'He must be very cross with us, he's charging down on top of us.
A cross-with-us rhinoceros! But why?'

'Gosh!' said Willy. 'Oooh!' said Wally.
Tilly stammered, 'G-g-golly! G-g-goodness! M-m-me oh my!'
'Come on,' I called, 'no time for that. Let's run before we're all squashed flat.'
Willy wailed, 'I wish that we could fly.'

With the rhino behind Willy,

And Willy behind Tilly, and Tilly behind Wally behind me;
We hurtled headlong through the grass, that rhino gaining on us fast,

Until we found a safe and sturdy tree.

Up we scrambled, up we hurried,
Up and up and up we scurried.
Up we fled for all that we were worth,

While that cross-with-us rhinoceros
Sniffed and snuffed and snorted,
As he stomped his rough, round feet into the earth.

Willy wept. Wally moaned.
'How long will we be here?' he groaned.

Poor Tilly was so scared she couldn't speak.
Then, looking down, I noticed

That the cross-with-us rhinoceros
Had lain down in the sun and gone to sleep.

Down we crept, while he slept.
We thought that we'd escape,
But as we tiptoed quickly off

We heard that rhino wake.

The thunder started up again, the thunder of those feet,
And closer, ever closer, came that dreadful, drumming beat.
We scuttled up a nearby hill

And down the other side.

There we saw a sight which made us all go weak inside.
A river deep. A river wide. I cried, 'We just can't win!'
'Why?' you ask. I'll tell you why: none of us could swim.

We closed our eyes.
Was this the end?
We had nowhere to go.

But then we heard that rhino stop,
Yes, STOP, and say, 'Hello.'

That cross-with-us rhinoceros, he stopped and said, 'Hello.'
A cross-with-us rhinoceros would never behave so.
Clearly that rhinoceros was never, ever cross with us.

'I followed you,' he said, 'to be your friend.'
'Why, how nice,' we cried as one. He took us riding in the sun.
And so our story had a happy end.

Some bestselling Red Fox picture books

THE BIG ALFIE AND ANNIE ROSE STORYBOOK
by Shirley Hughes
OLD BEAR
by Jane Hissey
OI! GET OFF OUR TRAIN
by John Burningham
DON'T DO THAT!
by Tony Ross
NOT NOW, BERNARD
by David McKee
ALL JOIN IN
by Quentin Blake
THE WHALES' SONG
by Gary Blythe and Dyan Sheldon
JESUS' CHRISTMAS PARTY
by Nicholas Allan
THE PATCHWORK CAT
by Nicola Bayley and William Mayne
WILLY AND HUGH
by Anthony Browne
THE WINTER HEDGEHOG
by Ann and Reg Cartwright
A DARK, DARK TALE
by Ruth Brown
HARRY, THE DIRTY DOG
by Gene Zion and Margaret Bloy Graham
DR XARGLE'S BOOK OF EARTHLETS
by Jeanne Willis and Tony Ross
WHERE'S THE BABY?
by Pat Hutchins